Cocktails

100 Non-Alcoholic Cocktails

by Barbara O'neill

How to Make Cocktails

You can make a lot of combinations of cocktails.

It's easy to make. All you need is fresh produce (fruit, vegetables, herbs, spices), water or juice. Choose what you want. Wash, chop your produce and mix.

Some produce will add flavor immediately, other produce will soak longer.

The end-product should be stored at room temperature for about two hours.
Then put it in the refrigerator.
I recommend peeling the citrus peel because the drink will be bitter.

You can make cocktails with any number of herbs, spices, fruit and vegetables!

Use thin slices or small cubes because the flavor will infuse more quickly.

Let's start!

1

ice cubes   orange juice   caramel syrop   espresso coffee   orange

2

lime   crushed ice   mint   sugar syrup   soda water

3

grenadine   crushed ice   lemon juice   strawberry syrup   strawberry

peach juice

4

roasted peanuts   milk   vanilla ice cream   caramel syrop

5

sugar syrup   apple juice   tarragon   kiwi   sprite

ice cubes

6

red grapes   pineapple juice   coconut syrup   banana   ice cubes

7

chocolate syrup   milk   chocolate ice cream

8

grapefruit   grapefruit juice   sugar syrup   ice cubes

9

strawberry   milk   strawberry ice cream

10

sugar syrup   soda water   lemon   mint   ice cubes

11

tangerine syrup   tangerine   mint   soda water   lime

crushed ice

12

grenadine   lemon juice   soda water   blueberry   blackberry

raspberry   strawberry   crushed ice

13

orange juice   mango   passion fruit   lemon juice   water without gas

14

grenadine   peach juice   apple   crushed ice   cocktail red cherry

15

espresso coffee   milk   ice cubes   whipped cream   chocolate syrup

16

honey   rosemary   cucumber   orange   lime

crushed ice   sprite

17

honey   raspberry   soda water   lemon zest   granulated sugar

18

mint   strawberry syrup   lime   strawberry   water without gas

19

mango   lemon juice   ginger syrup   mint   ice cubes

20

apple   apple juice   ice cubes   vanilla syrup   sugar syrup

lime juice

21

passion fruit syrup   coconut purée   milk   whipped cream

22

mint   crushed ice   lime juice   blackcurrant   cherry juice

blackcurrant syrup

23

coconut milk   pineapple juice   vanilla sugar   ice cubes   passion fruit

---

24

almond syrup   espresso coffee   milk   crushed ice   ice cubes

---

25

honey syrup   orange juice   ice cubes   lemon juice   orange

tangerine juice

26

water without gas   mint   honey   grated nutmeg   lime

ice cubes

27

sugar syrup   sprite   strawberry   mint   ginger root

28

sprite   lemon juice   rose syrup   vanilla sugar   ice cubes

29

sugar syrup   honey syrup   lemon juice   soda water   ginger root

pear   ice cubes

30

strawberry syrup   apple juice   soda water   vanilla syrup   lime juice

31

sugar syrup   lime juice   orange juice   soda water   passion fruit

ice cubes

32

lemon juice   pineapple juice   strawberry   orange juice   raspberry

33

sugar syrup   lime juice   red basil   soda water   cucumber

34

strawberry   honey   raspberry   lime juice   blackberry

cranberry juice   crushed ice

35

honey syrup   apple syrup   soda water   ginger root   grapefruit juice

36

blackcurrant syrup

apple juice

honey

pineapple juice

crushed ice

37

grenadine

water without gas

clove

ground cinnamon

lemon

orange

vanilla sugar

38

raspberry syrup

soda water

raspberry

lime

crushed ice

39

blackcurrant syrup

lime

tangerine juice

water without gas

grapefruit

ice cubes

40

raspberry syrup

raspberry

mint

lemon

sprite

41

strawberry syrup

cranberry juice

apple juice

lemon

crushed ice

42

soda water

apple ice cream

lime

honey

apple

ground cinnamon

vanilla sugar

43

sugar syrup

lime juice

apple juice

cucumber

pear

44

spirulina

pineapple

pineapple juice

crushed ice

45

passion fruit syrup

cucumber

mango

tangerine juice

soda water

ice cubes

46

sugar syrup   vanilla syrup   orange juice   watermelon   sprite

47

sugar syrup   lime juice   water without gas   honey   lemon

apple   ground nutmeg

48

maple syrup   lemon   honey   apple   linden tea

vanilla sugar   crushed ice

49

raspberry syrup   lemon juice   sprite   ice cubes   red basil

50

coconut syrup   lemon juice   cucumber   soda water   green basil

51

| milk | blackberry ice cream | blackberry | granulated sugar | vanilla sugar |

52

| honey syrup | water without gas | lemon juice | strawberry | raspberry |

53

| milk | raspberry | honey | granulated sugar | vanilla sugar |

quail egg yolk

54

| milk | raspberry | blueberry | vanilla sugar | raspberry ice cream |

55

| passion fruit syrup | lemon juice | soda water | watermelon | granulated sugar |

ice cubes   cinnamon

56

| blackcurrant syrup | soda water | lemon juice | blackcurrant | cinnamon |

57

| cranberry | raspberry | milk | honey | raspberry ice cream |

58

| milk | banana | vanilla sugar | banana ice cream |

59

| lemon | vanilla sugar | orange juice | orange | pear |

ice cubes

60

| grenadine | pineapple | lemon | mint | pineapple ice cream |

61

apple juice   kiwi ice cream   kiwi

62

cherry syrup   apple juice   cherry juice   cinnamon   ice cubes

---

63

sugar syrup   milk   honey   banana   kiwi

apple   raspberry   cherry   gooseberry

64

chocolate syrup   milk   cinnamon   crushed ice   banana

65

orange juice   vanilla sugar   mango   clove   crushed ice

66

granulated sugar   yogurt   blueberry   vanilla syrup   cinnamon

67

milk   blueberry ice cream   blueberry

68

dates   banana   milk   crushed ice

69

melon juice   honey   water without gas   lime juice   ice cubes

ginger root

70

watermelon   granulated sugar   lemon   vanilla sugar   mint

ice cubes   water without gas

71

mint   banana   honey   water without gas   apple

ice cubes

72

caramel syrop   orange   banana   tangerine juice   ice cubes

73

lime   mint   honey   soda water   ice cubes

74

pineapple juice   pineapple   blueberry   vanilla ice cream

75

pomegranate juice   peach   ice cubes   red grapes   orange

76

| strawberry juice | orange juice | strawberry | vanilla sugar | ice cubes |

77

| grenadine | pineapple juice | blackberry | orange juice | lemon juice |

| strawberry | apple | ice cubes |

78

| sugar syrup | grapefruit juice | grapefruit | cinnamon | ice cubes |

79

| sugar syrup | cranberry | clove | soda water | ice cubes |

80

| blackberry syrup | water without gas | apple juice | lemon juice | blackberry |

| ice cubes | rosemary |

18

81

sprite lemon lime lemon juice grapefruit juice

ice cubes pear

82

grape juice lemon apple peach ice cubes

83

kiwi lemon crushed ice watermelon

84

sea buckthorn syrup cinnamon grapefruit ginger root honey

ice cubes soda water

85

strawberry mint lime sprite crushed ice

86

milk   vanilla ice cream   vanilla syrup   honey   clove

87

honey syrup   banana   watermelon   strawberry   blueberry

ice cubes   vanilla sugar

88

cranberry juice   blueberry   raspberry   cherry   crushed ice

89

blackcurrant syrup   lime   orange   soda water   grapefruit

ice cubes   cinnamon

90

melon juice   honey   apple   pear   ice cubes

91 milk · honey · raspberries · figs · crushed ice

92 milk · mint · vanilla sugar · granulated sugar · ice cubes

93 strawberry syrup · water without gas · strawberry · mint · honey

94 oatmeal · milk · dried apricot · raisins · honey

vanilla sugar · crushed ice

95 peach · strawberry · mango · peach juice · vanilla syrup

ice cubes · ginger root

96

| apple juice | vanilla syrup | honey | apple | soda water |

97

sugar syrup | vanilla sugar | vanilla ice cream | milk | nutmeg

98

orange juice | peach | honey | nectarine | mint

soda water | crushed ice

99

milk | crushed ice | halva | plum

100

lemon | water without gas | apple | ice cubes | pear

honey | mango juice

22

Bon appetit!

Content

Made in United States
Troutdale, OR
10/30/2023

14149389R00017